This book is a gift to:

From:

Date:

Anna-Maré Ackermann

Let me pray too

40 prayers for infants and toddlers

CHRISTIAN
ART
PUBLISHERS

Originally published by Christian Publishing Company
under the title *Ek wil ook bid*

CHRISTIAN ART PUBLISHERS
P O Box 1599, Vereeniging, 1930

First edition 2001

Translated by Anna-Maré Ackermann
Original illustrations by Annaleen Conradie
Adapted to full colour illustrations by Christian Art Publishers for this edition
Cover designed by Christian Art Publishers

Set in 26 on 29 pt Kidprint by Christian Art Publishers

Printed in Singapore

ISBN 1-86852-806-5

01 02 03 04 05 06 07 08 09 10 – 10 9 8 7 6 5 4 3 2 1

CONTENTS

Preface

This book had its origin when my daughter-in-law, Connie, saw the lack of suchlike books when she was looking for a book with prayers for Conré and asked me to write a book for toddlers and primary pupils.

I am grateful that it could result in a publication, and it was a pleasure to use this talent to the glory of God.

Many thanks to Conré's other grandma, Annaleen, who gave this book life with her special illustrations.

Dedicated to my grandson Conré.

GENERAL

1

Jesus, I love you.
Help me live a life that's true.

AMEN

2

Jesus, keep me in your arm
where I'm safe and where I'm calm.

AMEN

3

Jesus, let me praise your name
you will always be the same.

AMEN

4

Jesus, when I go by car
be with me, near or far.

AMEN

5

Jesus, help me keep my mood
always gentle, always good.

AMEN

6

Thank you, Jesus, for my nose,
for ten fingers and ten toes.

AMEN

7

Thank you, Jesus, I'm not sick.
I can run and I can kick.

AMEN

8

Jesus, I look up to Thee.
Open my eyes, so I may see.

AMEN

9

Jesus, will you hold my hand
and all the children's in our land.

AMEN

10

Jesus, help me share my toys
with other little girls and boys.

AMEN

11

Jesus, forgive all my sins today.
That's why I always have to pray.

AMEN

12

Forgive my sins, dear Jesus, do,
for you are my kind Saviour too.

AMEN

13

Thank you, Jesus, for teaching me
that all good things come from Thee.

AMEN

14

Thank you, Jesus, that what I achieve
is only blessings which I receive.
It's mercy alone from up above,
surrounded by your lasting love.

AMEN

15

Jesus, you are very kind.
You died for us, you didn't mind.
Let us remember day by day
that for our sins, you had to pay.

AMEN

16

Jesus, you are always true
with everything you say or do.
Forgive my sins for I am weak,
make me strong, but keep me meek.

AMEN

17

Jesus, keep us kind and humble,
hold our hand, so we won't stumble.
Lead us daily wherever we go,
be with us in want and woe.

AMEN

18

Gentle Jesus, help me stay
safe and sound by night and day.
Keep me from the bad and wrong,
let me praise you with a song.

AMEN

19

Jesus, remember and don't forget
when I fall and tears are shed.
Keep me on the narrow road,
help me with my heavy load.

AMEN

20

Jesus, thank you that I know
you are there and love me so.
I know that I will never regret
listening to all that you have said.

AMEN

21

Jesus, I kneel because I am meek
and pray that forgiveness I may seek.
Thank you for everything I receive.
What more could I do, but just believe.

AMEN

22

Jesus, forgive me every day,
because I keep on going astray.
Help me to be honest and sincere,
faithful and humble, without any fear.

AMEN

23

For food and clothes, I thank you
and all the things I can do,
for arms and legs to run and play,
to share whatever comes my way.

AMEN

FAMILY AND FRIENDS

24

Jesus, bless my mommy dear,
Jesus, bless my daddy dear.

AMEN

25

Thank you, Jesus, for all my grandpa's.
Thank you, Jesus, for all my grandma's.

AMEN

26

Thank you, Jesus, that I may pray
for family near or far away.

AMEN

27

Thank you, Jesus, for my teacher I adore.
I love her, but I love you more.

AMEN

28

Thank you for my mom and dad.
They taught me the difference between
good and bad.
They also taught me to start each day
by reading the Bible and to pray.

AMEN

29

Jesus, be with my friend and I.
Don't let us sin and tell a lie.
Let us love and keep your commands
and not give in to sly demands.

AMEN

30

Jesus, thank you for our native land,
for mountains, rivers, sea and sand.
For giving us a special friend
to share your love without an end.

AMEN

GRACE AT MEALS

31

Thank you Jesus, that we may share this food and be of your presence aware.

AMEN

32

Bless this food, O Lord, we ask, help us with our daily task.

AMEN

33

Jesus, we give thanks to you
for food and other good things too.

AMEN

34

Thank you for food which comes from above,
for health and blessings and for your love.

AMEN

35

Before we eat we ask you to bless
this food and think of those who have less.
Thank you that we have food every day
and for all the blessings on our way.

AMEN

36

Thank you, Jesus, for food we get,
that every day, we are fed.
Lead us on the rightful way,
keep us thankful every day.

AMEN

NATURE

37

Thank you, Jesus, for flowers and
trees,
for animals, birds and little bees.

AMEN

38

Thank you, Jesus, for grass so green,
for rain that washes all so clean.

AMEN

39

Thank you, Jesus, for the sun
that shines so warm on everyone.

AMEN

40

Thank you, Jesus, for the sun
that lights the day for everyone,
for moon and stars twinkling bright,
for guarding us by day and night.

AMEN